THE
AWAKENING
SOUL

HAROLD KLEMP

ECKANKAR

Minneapolis

www.Eckankar.org

ABOUT THIS BOOK: *The Awakening Soul* is compiled from Harold Klemp's writings. These selections originally appeared in his books published by Eckankar.

The Awakening Soul

Copyright © 2012 ECKANKAR

The terms ECKANKAR, ECK, EK, MAHANTA, and SOUL TRAVEL, among others, are trademarks of ECKANKAR, PO Box 2000, Chanhassen, MN 55317-2000 USA. 120401

Printed in USA
Compiled by Joan Klemp
Edited by Patrick Carroll, Joan Klemp, and Anthony Moore
Cover photo by Connie Kroskin
Author photo by Robert Huntley
Cover design by Doug Munson

Library of Congress Cataloging-in-Publication Data

Klemp, Harold.
  The awakening soul / Harold Klemp.
     p. cm.
  Summary: "Author Harold Klemp, spiritual leader of Eckankar, gives inspiration to help you enhance your creativity, solve problems, and see the spiritual opportunities in your everyday life"--Provided by publisher.
  ISBN 978-1-57043-380-1 (alk. paper)
  1. Eckankar (Organization) 2. Spiritual life--Eckankar (Organization)   I. Title.
  BP605.E3K5465 2007
  299'.93--dc23
                                        2012028622

♾ This paper meets the requirements of ANSI/NISO Z39.48-1992 (Permanence of Paper).

Contents

DEAR READER

The awakening Soul is on the path to enlightenment. "Enlightenment," says Harold Klemp, "is a gentle thing if it's right, if you're ready for it."

You, as Soul, a divine particle of God, learn to open your wings through experience. The lessons of life act like the chrysalis the humble caterpillar must pass through before becoming the elegant butterfly.

Your grace will be recognized by others as you become the awakening Soul. You grow in your capacity to love, establishing the correct relationship between you and God.

"Then you're able to go back out into the world," says the author, "and serve all God's creatures. And you will serve with love, kindness, compassion, and understanding."

Contemplate just one quote each day. Draw from the well of God-knowledge within you. As you apply this wisdom to your everyday life, you soar. You inspire those around you to awaken and to soar as well!

THE
TEACHER

*E*arth is a classroom that brings about the spiritual maturity of Soul.

*S*oul enters this world to accomplish a collection of tasks. Taken as a whole, these assignments make up Its destiny.

*T*he purpose of life is to give Soul—
and that means you—an education so It can
become a Co-worker with God.

*T*rue service to God is always an adventure in learning spiritual things.

When God's love comes to you,
it must work through you.

*L*ife has a way of teaching us better.

*E*very experience, waking or dream,

has a lesson or message to impart to us.

*W*hatever you are going through today is training for tomorrow.

You need today to reach tomorrow.

The tests of Spirit are unlimited.
They reach you in a totally unique way.

*O*ur mates, friends, fellow workers, strangers, and more, all join the march of time.

Each is our greatest teacher at some point.

We learn very soon that no matter what happens to us, the purpose is to teach us more about the laws of Divine Spirit.

CREATIVITY

*L*ife is a mystery until we come to the path of ECK (Divine Spirit) and begin to understand that we can be the creators of our own world.

*S*oul can create whatever it needs.

Soul, a particle of God, is blessed with the gift of creative imagination, which finds a solution for every problem.

The creative imagination gives us a way to make our dreams come true.

*W*orking with the creative power of Soul means learning how to focus your attention.

The cycle of creative action begins with the concept we carry in our minds of what we wish to do.

The creative power works best through those who love what they are doing.

What we are trying to achieve is the upliftment of spiritual consciousness through our creative abilities.

We're using our creativity to learn how to work with Divine Spirit, how to come into harmony with life around us.

How does one live the spiritual life? The answer is simply to live creatively, because each of us is working to become a Co-worker with God.

*B*eing a Co-worker with God means continuing to develop—not just your creative powers, but your capacity to love.

GRACEFUL LIVING

*G*race is a balm that makes things run better.

*T*hrough our experiences here on earth, Soul develops the beauty and grace It needs to become a Co-worker with God.

When you are with others, realize they too are lights of God trying to find their way home to a better, happier, more graceful life.

As Souls unfold, their way of interacting with others becomes more graceful.

*L*ife is a jungle, but it is likewise a garden. It provides a time and place for unfoldment, because Soul is tempered by hardship.

*T*he daily struggles that life presents
are opportunities to cultivate spiritual grace.

*B*efore you can improve your life and find a measure of happiness, you must learn to do one thing every day out of pure love.

We look for ways to make things better for our loved ones, ourselves, and others. Life is for giving and loving, which fosters the nobility of spirit.

*S*eek the highest, and the rest of life will fall into place.

$\mathcal{G}$raceful living, being gracious, means that you are filled with the blessings of God. And if you are filled with the blessings of God, you will certainly live gracefully and graciously with others.

*G*ive your best effort each day, and leave the rest to ECK, the Holy Spirit.

$\mathcal{B}$ LESSINGS

What is the greatest blessing? The gift of life itself.

*G*od's blessings are always with you. You just need the eyes to see and the ears to hear.

*E*verything is a gift from God. The challenge is to understand what is happening to you.

If we take responsibility and do something that gives us greater understanding, life becomes easier.

A turning point is life's way of giving you a chance to move ahead spiritually, though you must reach for the gift yourself.

When one asks in sincerity "What is love?" and opens his heart, the ECK (Divine Spirit) will bring the gift that is already there and has been all along.

$\mathcal{L}$ook for the blessing.

The person who is causing us the most trouble is also giving us a chance to learn the most about ourselves spiritually.

*W*e serve God and life out of gratitude. Why? For the blessings we have received.

True contemplation is reflecting on the blessings of God in your life.

If you can just stop and be grateful for the blessings that are before you, your heart will open to love.

Then the blessings can keep coming.

And as we bless this day, we realize it was another opportunity to grow: to see, to know, to be.

THANKSGIVING

$\mathcal{G}$ive thanks for the gift of life.

*O*pen your eyes to the miracles around you: your friends, your good fortunes, for all that life has seen fit to send your way.

*T*oday comes but once. Recognize its goodness. Open your heart.

*Y*ou are Soul. Special. One of a kind. So love yourself, love God, and love others.

Look around and say thank you for all the blessings.

*T*hanksgiving is one of the attributes or qualities that come to the person who loves God.

One who loves God loves life. This love bestows protection and gratitude upon an individual.

When love is on the field, fear must retreat.

*B*egin with the love you have. Love gratefully. This love expands your heart into a greater vessel which can hold yet more love.

*L*ife will be more rewarding when we learn the secret of gratitude.

*O*ne who is thankful for every good thing will find the richness of heaven in the humblest detail of his spiritual life.

*T*he window of gratitude opens us to the heavens of God.

$\mathcal{S}$INGING
HU

How do you let the Spirit of God into your life? The simplest and best way is to sing HU, the age-old song of love for God.

$\mathcal{H}$U is a spiritual exercise or a prayer.

*A*s you sing HU (sounds like the word *hue*, but drawn out), you're simply saying, "Thy will be done."

We don't try to tell God what to do. We listen to hear what God's Voice is saying to us.

*I*f you sing HU every day for ten minutes, filling your heart with as much love as you can, you will find a greater awareness of the factors affecting your survival, both here on earth and on the inner planes.

*H*U will put a fresh, new spirit into your life. You will begin to be a happier person, because It will show you what things are truly important for you and what are not.

*I*f you know how to sing HU, you can open yourself to the Holy Spirit. You can open yourself to the help that It's offering you to help you take the next step.

There is a saying that there are really no secret teachings, that everything we need to know is available to us on an open shelf somewhere. But it depends upon our state of consciousness to accept it.

*T*ake questions to the Inner Master. Chant a sacred word, such as the name for God, HU, and ask for answers to come in the best way.

The Inner Master and the ECK, Holy Spirit, are one and the same.

*I*f you're in trouble, in pain, in need of comfort, or in need of love, sing HU quietly to yourself.

*S*ing HU, and, in your mind and heart, watch this quiet stream of God's love flow gently into your heart and being.

HU opens your heart to God. It opens you to God's sweet love.

*S*hould the worlds tremble and all else fail, HU carries us into the ocean of God's love and mercy.

SPIRITUAL HEALING

The process of spiritual healing teaches us something about ourselves we didn't know before.

*M*ost of our problems are self-made.

When the eyes are in trouble, we have to ask, What am I *not* seeing about my spiritual life that is causing me difficulty with my eyesight?

*O*ften it takes pain and necessity before we say, My eyes are open. I'm looking.

Then when the blessings—the different methods of healing—show up, we recognize them as the next step.

A solution exists for every challenge to our peace of mind. There is always a way, somehow.

All the help that comes to us is from the Holy Spirit, whether it comes in a dream or through the help of a friend or doctor.

*T*he trick is the discrimination you need to tell what's good for you and what's not.

This comes by listening to your heart.

*T*he key is to stay in tune with Divine Spirit. Through the Spiritual Exercises of ECK, you can be aware of the hints and nudges of the Holy Spirit as It tries to guide you to the next step to take.

*H*ere is a way to help yourself that begins with a spiritual exercise.

At bedtime, softly sing HU, this ancient name for God, for five to ten minutes.

*T*hen see a mental picture of your problem as a simple cartoon. Beside it place an image of the condition as you feel it should be. Now go to sleep as usual.

*U*pon awakening, make a short note about any dreams you recall.

Also be alert during the day for clues about your problem from other people. The Holy Spirit works through them too.

*W*hen troubles or worries spring up, try to fill yourself with love and ask, "What lesson is the divine ECK, Holy Spirit, giving me in this to make me a better, more whole spiritual being?"

GIVING

*F*acing life gracefully is probably the first step to giving of yourself to others.

The purpose of life is to become a
Co-worker with God. It means service to
others, using our talents and interests to give
hand, ear, or heart to another in need.

We try to express the love of God through who we are and how we live.

*L*ove God, and let others love God in their own way too. Set the example of what it means to be a lover of God.

When our hearts are open to God's love, then the divine power can use us as an instrument to pass divine love and blessings along to others.

If you want to bring yourself closer to the Holy Spirit, say, "I am a vehicle for God and Divine Spirit." Then begin your day with joy. Know that everything is being accomplished as it should be.

We have to go out into the world and give of ourselves, but not in a gushy, emotional way. Instead, we give true service to others in the way that they need at the moment.

So what have I to give? you ask. Often it's as simple as patience, love, and understanding.

*O*nce you've established the correct relationship between yourself and God, then you're able to go back out into the world and serve all God's creatures. And you will serve with love, kindness, compassion, and understanding.

This is the whole purpose of Soul studying the teachings of ECK: to become a Co-worker with God. To serve life out of love, because of gratitude for the gift of life.

*D*o what you can for yourself. Do what you can for others. In doing so, you are moving forward spiritually as a divine light of God.

CONSECRATION

$\mathcal{C}$onsecration means to make or declare sacred. It is dedicating yourself and all you do, say, think, and feel to God.

*P*eople on the path to God some-
times forget to consecrate themselves, to
make themselves holy, either by prayer,
meditation, or contemplation.

*W*hat you can do is recognize that
you are sacred and accept yourself as a child
of God.

*E*CK is the path of love. It exists to bring each of us to a greater state of love.

*W*hat is the spiritual purpose of life?

To learn to give and to receive love.

*L*ove the breath of air, for it's a gift of life. Love your work: It will expand your God-given powers of creation. And love and serve your dear ones.

*T*he lessons of life are purifying us to make us better beings, to make us better people.

*Y*ou face each problem that comes along, digging ever deeper into your resources. As you do this, you learn to work more fully in the spiritual arena with the Inner Master to find out how to resolve each new situation.

The Inner Master is just the inner form of Spirit, of the ECK, Holy Spirit.

*T*he answers can always be found at the inner temple. You have the source, the divine ECK, within your heart.

Approach the altar of God with love and humility, and your answers will come when all preparations have been made.

*E*nlightenment is a gentle thing if it's right, if you're ready for it. It gives you a different state of consciousness.

*L*ove is the only way to God. The only way. If you want to go this route, ask in contemplation to be shown the way.

THE LIGHT
AND SOUND

*D*ivine love is the Holy Spirit, God's love sent down to earth.

Spirit will work with each one of you in a way that is right for you.

*T*he Light and Sound are the two aspects through which the ECK, or Holy Spirit, makes Itself known. It comes in many forms to bring upliftment, comfort when we are troubled, or protection when we are in danger.

*T*hat Light and Sound—which means anything that you can see, anything that you can hear in your world—is the expression of God's love for you.

Experiences in the Sound and Light of God accelerate Soul's unfoldment.

*T*he HU Song, singing a holy name for God, sets these spiritual experiences into motion.

*T*he inner experiences occur more often and with more vividness in ECK than in possibly any other spiritual path on earth, because this teaching has the Light and Sound as living elements.

*T*he love of God comes through the Light and Sound.

The Light and Sound of God are food for Soul, and Soul cannot live without these two aspects of God coming into the core of Its being every day.

*A*s you receive more of the Sound and Light of ECK, you get greater responsibility along with the greater freedom.

To see the Light and hear the Sound is to experience spiritual upliftment that pulls you into the worlds of knowing.

*H*ere you become aware, consciously, of the divine laws of Spirit and can use this knowledge to wend your way through life, stepping carefully among the rocks that have been thrown there to stub your toe.

*E*ach of us must someday become the Sound and Light, for in them alone is found the way to God.

That is the road to Mastership.

Soul's Mission

Each of you has a spiritual purpose
for coming into this lifetime.

The purpose of the spiritual path of ECK is to give you an idea of how to become a more spiritual being and master your spiritual destiny.

To master your spiritual destiny, you at least have to be aware of what the five passions of the mind are.

Any of these passions—lust, anger, greed, attachment, and vanity—are simply just too much of a good thing.

*T*here are also five virtues—ways to offset the passions: discrimination, forgiveness or tolerance, contentment, detachment, and humility.

*E*CK is the path of moderation. I've put together five points that may help you day to day.

*P*oint number one: Forget the past
and learn the spiritual lessons of today.

The second point: Look for a new way to solve a stubborn problem.

*P*oint number three: Whatever you undertake, do it to the best of your ability. If necessary, do it even better.

*P*oint number four: Being different can make you an outcast or a leader. Some-time you need to make a choice.

*P*oint number five: Tell others about the teachings of ECK.

This ties in with the greater spiritual purpose, why Soul has come here: to become a Co-worker with God.

*T*o become a Co-worker with God is the main mission each Soul is trying to accomplish.

WAY OF THE ETERNAL

Each must make his own way to truth, on his own path and in his own time.

*T*he route of this quest is both a unique and solitary one. Yet all creation awaits the awakening of each individual Soul.

The teachings of ECK work on the simple principle that love is the divine current which makes all life possible.

ECK is the Holy Spirit, and It pervades everything with Its presence. ECK is the Spirit of life.

You, as a channel for Divine Spirit, often touch people. Because of you, changes occur in them which allow their lives to be made better.

But it works only to the degree that you can step back and let the inner power work through you. The inner power is love.

*H*U is the love song to God that we sing. And it's to open your heart—like opening your wings. Opening your wings simply means opening your state of consciousness.

The way to heaven is told to us in the ECK scriptures, the Shariyat-Ki-Sugmad, which means the "Way of the Eternal." But the actual working out of this high destiny is done in the privacy of your contemplation.

The secret doctrine is the portion of the Shariyat-Ki-Sugmad that the Inner Master passes to you by means of the Spiritual Exercises of ECK.

This is the road to God all spiritual travelers take to Mastership.

When we speak of opening your wings, it's coming into an awareness of the spiritual love and protection of the ECK Masters.

These spiritual travelers are the guardian angels around you all the time.

An ECK Master, like a good teacher, will teach you the lessons most able to help you lead a happy and useful spiritual life.

*F*ind out for yourself. This is what the teachings of ECK are prepared to help you do.

ABOUT THE AUTHOR

Author Harold Klemp is known as a pioneer of today's focus on "everyday spirituality." He was raised on a Wisconsin farm and attended divinity school. He also served in the US Air Force.

In 1981, after years of training, he became the spiritual leader of Eckankar, Religion of the Light and Sound of God. His mission is to help people find their way back to God in this life.

Harold Klemp speaks each year to thousands of seekers at Eckankar seminars. Author of more than seventy-five books, he continues to write, including many articles and spiritual-study discourses. Harold Klemp's inspiring and practical approach to spirituality helps thousands of people worldwide find greater freedom, wisdom, and love in their lives.

ALSO BY
HAROLD KLEMP

*Available at bookstores, from online booksellers,
or directly from:*
Eckankar
PO Box 2000, Chanhassen, MN 55317-2000 USA.
Tel (952) 380-2222 Fax (952) 380-2196
www.Eckankar.org

Immortality of Soul Series
The Language of Soul
Love—The Keystone of Life
Truth Has No Secrets
Touching the Face of God
The Awakened Heart
HU, the Most Beautiful Prayer
The Loving Heart
The Spiritual Life

A selected list:
The Call of Soul
The Spiritual Exercises of ECK
The Spiritual Laws of Life
Past Lives, Dreams, and Soul Travel
Those Wonderful ECK Masters